D0916851

GREAT MYSTERIES OF THE AIR

Edward F. Dolan, Jr. *(handwritten: FRANCIS)* *(handwritten: 1924 –)*

Illustrated with photographs
and drawings

DODD, MEAD & COMPANY
NEW YORK

PICTURE CREDITS

United Press International Photo, 26, 31, 55, 59, 65, 69, 70, 72, 74, 82, 84, 112; Official U.S. Navy Photograph, 53, 62, 101, 105, 122. Drawings by Richard B. Lyttle, 19, 21, 44. Maps on pages 87 and 99 are by the author.

Library of Congress Cataloging in Publication Data

Dolan, Edward F., date
   Great mysteries of the air.

   Includes index.
   Summary: Presents unsolved mysteries of modern
flight, including ghostly appearances, unexplained
crashes, and aircraft disappearances.
   1. Aeronautics — Miscellanea — Juvenile literature.
[1. Aeronautics — Miscellanea] I. Title.
TL547.D64   1983   629.13'09   83-8946
ISBN 0-396-08185-1

For Betsy and Grant

CONTENTS

INTRODUCTION
Mysteries 9

1 The Ghost of Planes of World War II 12

2 The Ghosts of Eastern Airlines 25

3 The Mystery Clouds 40

4 What Happened to Airship L-8? 52

5 They Disappeared 67

6 The Vanished Electra 81

7 The Deadly Triangle 96

8 Are There Answers? 111

Index 125

Introduction

MYSTERIES

Three fighter planes took off from an Air Force base in 1950. They flew in formation out over a bay. Suddenly, they nosed over and plunged into the water. All at the same time, their engines had quit.

What caused the three engines to stall at the same moment? No one knows. It seems that they stopped for no reason at all. The incident remains a mystery to this day.

It's a real puzzler. But it's just one of many. Our century is often called the century of flight. It might also be called the century of the great mysteries of the air.

Ever since the beginning of time, we humans have wanted to fly with the birds. We first broke free of the earth in the balloons of the eighteenth and nineteenth centuries. But true flight — the sort that can take us quickly from place to place — did not come until the birth of the engine-powered airplane in 1903. The engine-powered plane was improved over the years and now enables us to go wherever we please in the sky. Giant jet airliners carry us across the world. Small private planes give us hours of flying pleasure. And rockets are beginning to take us to the stars.

But, no matter how easily it can get us from place to place, the airplane still finds the skies to be a strange place. One mysterious happening after another has found its way into the history of aviation. Planes have flown into clouds and then, for no known reason, have dropped out with their wings torn away. Planes have disappeared on long and short hops, never to be found. Planes have vanished from the sky, sometimes when they were within sight of busy areas. There have been several airliners with ghosts aboard them. And there have been planes that were themselves ghosts.

In this book, we're going to look at some of the best of these mysteries. They add up to a puzzling—and sometimes scary—page in the story of modern flight. But don't look for any solutions to the mysteries. There aren't any. And there may never be.

Just enjoy being mystified. Let's start with some ghosts.

1

THE GHOST PLANES
OF WORLD WAR II

It was a moonlight night early in World War II. A fighter plane from Britain's Royal Air Force flew along the eastern coast of England. At the controls, the pilot swung his gaze from side to side. He was on a patrol mission. His job was to look out for German bombers.

Suddenly, the pilot's eyes narrowed. He peered hard into the night. There was a plane in the distance off to his side. He knew immediately that it wasn't a bomber. It was too small. But it puzzled him. He could barely see the ship in the moonlight. Yet it seemed to have a strange shape. It looked like no British or German aircraft that he had ever run into.

There was only one thing to do. The pilot had to take a closer look. He banked and dived toward the stranger. Whatever it was, it showed good speed. No matter where he flew, the little plane darted away and kept its distance. The pilot had never seen anything this odd before. He wondered if he had come upon a new and secret enemy weapon.

Then the strange ship flew across the face of the moon. Now the pilot could see it clearly in every detail. He grew more puzzled than ever.

The stranger was anything but a new and secret weapon. It was an airplane, all right. But it was an old one that didn't belong in World War II — a two-winger (a biplane) with an open cockpit. The pilot could see a helmeted head above the rim of the cockpit. Now he remembered something. As a boy, he had seen pictures of planes like this. They had fought long ago in World War I. They hadn't been made and flown for years now.

But the pilot saw that, indeed, it was an enemy ship. Painted on each wing was an Iron Cross. There was also an Iron Cross on the body of the plane. The Iron Cross! That was the insignia used by Germany back in World War I. The pilot was looking at a plane from another war — a war that had been fought more than twenty long years ago. It was impossible.

While the British pilot stared, the little plane with its Iron Cross insignia flew on and disappeared into the night. The British flyer continued on his patrol mission. But he was a bewildered and shaken man. He wondered if he had imagined the plane. He shook his head. No. It had definitely been there. Then that meant just one thing. A chill went down his spine.

He had been chasing after a ghost!

Ghosts?

Did the pilot really see a ghost? No one can say for sure because no one really knows whether there are such things as ghosts. There are, however, a great many people who believe in them. They feel sure that, after death, a human being goes on living as a spirit in the hereafter. They believe that this spirit is able to return to the world or send messages to us.

But there are others who scoff at all such talk. To them, ghosts are nonsense. They say that people who meet ghosts are just "seeing things." Or that the ghostly appearances are caused by a natural something — say, a mist rising from the ground. They also argue that some individuals can't handle their problems by themselves. They want to be helped by friends and loved ones from beyond the grave. Finally, they imagine that they can see and hear them.

Who is right? Who is wrong? There are no answers.

But one thing can be said for certain. The British pilot was *sure* that he had met a ghost. And so were many other flyers in World War II. The old German biplane wasn't the only ghost ship to be seen during the long years of fighting. At least three others were sighted.

Here are their stories.

Help from "Old Willie"

Royal Air Force pilots received some help from a ghost ship one night. They were out to stop a group of Heinkel bombers heading for London. Their Spitfire fighters drew near the enemy craft. Suddenly, they found an old-fashioned plane in their formation. It was the type of ship that the Canadians had flown during World War I. They could see the pilot in the open cockpit. They tried to signal him. He paid no attention.

As the Heinkels came closer, the old plane peeled away from the formation. It dove straight at the two leading bombers. They saw it coming. It gave no sign of turning aside, but seemed intent on crashing into them. The two bombers tried to swerve away to safety. They smashed into each other, burst into flames, and went spinning earthward.

The Canadian plane came out of its dive. It climbed back up to the British formation. The ghost pilot waved to the Spitfires—and then banked away and vanished into the night.

In the next months, many British flyers reported that the phantom pilot and his plane had helped them to down German bombers. His tactics, they said, were always the same. He would appear in their formation just as the enemy ships were sighted. Then he would dive straight at the two leading bombers. He'd force them to crash together. Or he'd frighten their pilots and make them easy targets for the British fighters.

The ghost pilot became so well known among Spitfire crews that they gave him a nickname—"Old Willie." They believed that he was the spirit of a Canadian pilot named Henshaw. It seems that Henshaw's greatest dream in World War I was to shoot down a German plane. It was a dream that never came true. Henshaw himself went down in flames during his first air battle. Badly wounded, he was sent home. For the rest of his life, he never stopped talking about his dream of old.

All the pilots who saw "Old Willie" were sure that Henshaw was making his dream come true in World War II — more than ten years after his death in 1929.

"The White Angel"

The fighter pilots weren't the only ones to find a friendly ghost in their midst. Bomber pilots — on both the German and British sides — also received help from the "great beyond." The German flyers sighted a ghost ship several times while on bombing runs during the battle to take the city of Warsaw in Poland. They called it "The White Angel of

"The White Angel" leads the way.

18

Warsaw" because it gave off a shimmering, ghostly light.

The "Angel" always appeared in the same way. As the bombers approached the city, the ship would suddenly appear in front of them. Shimmering and giving off its strange light, it would circle the city. It seemed to be pointing out their target for them. Then it would disappear and the bombers would begin their runs.

Warsaw finally fell to the Germans. From that time on, "The White Angel" was never seen again.

Meet "The Hot One"

The "Angel" had the job of guiding the German bombers to their targets. A British ghost was even more helpful. It warned the English bomber pilots of enemy gunfire up ahead.

"The Hot One" was a bomber from World War I. Yet in World War II, it helped British pilots by flying ahead of them and taking enemy antiaircraft fire.

They soon nicknamed it "The Hot One."

"The Hot One" was a giant Handley Page bomber from World War I. First built by the English in 1916, it had a wingspan of 100 feet and could carry a bomb load of 1,792 pounds. It was sent to bomb the factories in Germany's big industrial areas. As a ghost, it got back into action in World War II.

The ghost earned its nickname because of the way it warned of the enemy fire. The British bombers would be heading for their targets. Down below, hidden German guns would be taking aim on them. Then the big Handley Page would sweep into view. The pilots could see that no one was at the controls. The ghost would roar to the front — and the German guns would begin firing at it. Shrapnel would burst all about the plane. Chunks of metal would tear gaping holes in it.

Warned of the danger ahead, the bombers would swing safely away. Staying clear of the guns, they'd make their way to their target.

And what of the ghost? It would finish its

run through the enemy fire. Then it would bank clear, climb steeply, and disappear from view.

The ghost planes of World War II were seen by dozens of air crews on both sides of the fighting. But did the ghosts really exist? Did some helpful pilots really return from the hereafter to help their comrades? Or did the British and German flyers "see things"? Or did they so want help up there in the sky that they finally imagined it? The horror of war can play strange tricks on anyone's mind.

No one can answer these questions. But air crews are a sensible lot. They're not the types to "see things." Nor are they the types who would so want help that they would imagine that it was there. And, if they did want help, why would their minds call forth old planes from another war? Why not modern planes?

So who can say? Perhaps the pilots were actually getting help from the hereafter.

The pilots are certain that they had really

seen ghosts. So are all the people who lived through what may be the best ghost story in the history of aviation. It's the story of the ghosts of Eastern Airlines. Let's turn to it now.

2

THE GHOSTS OF
EASTERN AIRLINES

The brothers, Wilbur and Orville Wright, brought their airplane to the beach near Kitty Hawk, North Carolina. It was a flimsy-looking ship that they had built themselves. Its body was made of slender sticks. The wings were covered with linen cloth. But, with its 4-cylinder engine clattering, the plane bounced along the sands, lifted itself free, and sailed through the air one morning. It did the same thing four times before midday. Its best flight saw the plane soar for a distance of 852 feet. The date was an historic one — December 17, 1903. The Wrights had made the world's first

Orville and Wilbur Wright with their little plane on one of its historic flights in December of 1903.

flights in a powered aircraft. Those flights marked the birth of the age of aviation.

Almost seventy years later, a giant airliner passed close to the beach at Kitty Hawk. The ship was a Lockheed L-1011, powered by three Rolls-Royce jet engines. It was flying from New York's Kennedy International Airport to Miami International in Florida. On board this night of December 29, 1972, were 176 passengers and crew. Like the Wright Brothers' plane, the airliner was about to make history — but for an entirely different reason. It was about to give birth to the greatest aviation ghost story of our time.

The flight went smoothly that night. The air was calm. The lights of Miami came into view. The plane — it was called a Tri-star Whisperliner — began to drop down for a landing. It swept over the vast swamp area know as the Everglades. But the L-1011 never made it to the runway. It crashed into the Everglades, cutting a path 1,600 feet long before finally coming to rest.

The crash took the lives of 99 people. Seventy-seven survivors were rescued from the Everglades. Most of them suffered serious injuries.

Among the dead were two members of the flight crew. One was the plane's Captain. The other was the Flight Engineer. Both men lived through the crash, but died soon after. The Captain lived for about an hour. He was dead when rescuers finally removed him from the shattered flight deck. The Flight Engineer was taken to a hospital, only to die of his injuries about thirty hours later.

Ghostly Appearances

In the months following the crash, a number of strange incidents occurred. The Captain and the Flight Engineer were seen time and again. They appeared in ghostly form before pilots, flight officers, stewardesses, and passengers. The appearances took place aboard other L-1011s owned by Eastern Airlines. In particular, the ghosts were seen aboard an L-1011 listed in the company records as Plane 318.

Let's consider first the Captain's appearances.

One day, just before Plane 318 taxied out for a flight, the head stewardess took a final count of the passengers. She wanted to make sure that no one was missing. She found that there was an extra passenger on board — a man in the uniform of an Eastern pilot. The young woman went to his seat and tried to get his name. The stranger refused to talk. He even refused to look at her, but just sat there and stared straight ahead. The stewardess later said that he seemed to be in a daze.

Finally, the stewardess called for help. Another stewardess and the ship's pilot arrived at the seat. The pilot looked at the silent man and gasped. The passenger, he said, was the Captain whom he had known quite well.

At that moment, the Captain disappeared. He didn't get up and walk away. He simply vanished. Left behind were three very puzzled crewmembers.

On another occasion, a stewardess opened a luggage compartment above one of the seats. Her eyes widened. She had flown with the Captain some years earlier. Now she saw his face staring out at her from the compart-ment. The face vanished after a few moments.

The Flight Engineer made many more appearances than did the Captain. During one flight, a woman passenger was riding next to an empty seat. She glanced to her side — and was surprised to find a uniformed man sitting there. She had not seen him seat himself. She had no idea where he came from. He sat looking straight ahead. In the next instant, the woman was screaming. The stranger had vanished right before her eyes. Later, the woman was shown a photograph of the Flight Engineer. She identified him as the man in the empty seat.

One night, a crewmember went up to the flight deck to give it a final check before the pilot arrived for takeoff. He saw a man sitting at the engineering panel. He recognized the visitor immediately — the Flight Engineer. The crewman later said that the Engineer told him that he had just checked the panel and that it was in good working order. Then, as before,

The Lockheed L-1011 is known as one of the safest airliners ever built. The 1972 crash caused one of the greatest mysteries in aviation history.

the Flight Engineer disappeared.

Many of the Engineer's appearances took place in the galley below the passengers' cabin. It was lined with ovens used to heat the meals for everyone on board. The oven doors were equipped with small windows.

Several stewardesses, on looking through the windows, saw the Engineer's face reflected in the glass. One stewardess found an oven door open. She could see the Engineer's face within.

Another stewardess came into the galley during a night flight. She found the place clammy and cold, even though all the ovens were on. While unloading trays of food from the ovens, she felt as if someone were in the room with her. Then she caught sight of a ball of mist above the ovens. It was about the size of a grapefruit. She thought it might be caused by steam or condensation. But, as she watched, it grew to the size of a basketball. All the while, it shifted and changed shape. At last, it became the face of a man wearing glasses. The Flight Engineer had worn glasses.

A Helpful Ghost

In at least two of his appearances, the Flight Engineer proved to be a helpful ghost.

In midflight, a stewardess found that one of the ovens was not working properly. She telephoned the pilot and asked to have a crewman come and repair it. A man in a flight engineer's uniform appeared a few minutes later. He quickly took care of the problem and departed.

Then another engineer arrived. He looked puzzled when the stewardess explained that someone else had attended to things. He said that he was the only engineer on board. Later, the stewardess looked at the picture of the Flight Engineer. That was the man, she said, who had fixed the oven.

The Flight Engineer's most helpful appearance came during a trip that Plane 318 made to Mexico City. While down in the galley, a stewardess sighted his face in an oven window. Frightened, she hurried out. She told another stewardess of her experience. Together, they went to the galley. An officer from the flight deck joined them a short time later. The three stood and looked at the ghostly face. They could see it very clearly.

Its expression was troubled. At last, the ghost spoke. He warned them to watch out for the danger of fire aboard the plane.

The airliner made its way safely to Mexico City. But, when it took off for a return to the United States, one of its engines stalled. It began to backfire. There was an immediate danger of fire. The pilot quickly sidestepped the danger. He released a fire-fighting agent — carbon dioxide — into the stalled engine. Then he circled the airport and landed. Mechanics checked the engine. They could find no reason for the stall.

More Mystery

The ghost stories mystified everyone who heard them. Had the stewardesses and pilots really seen the ghostly appearances or had they imagined them?

On the one hand, it certainly seemed that they had seen *something*, no matter what it was. They were all trained airline workers who were noted for their calmness. Like the flyers who sighted the ghost ships of World War II, they weren't the types to "see things." And there had been times when the appearances had taken place in front of as many as three people. Each time, the people had all said that they had seen the same thing.

But, on the other hand, who could say what tricks the imagination might play on even the most sensible of individuals?

Adding to the mystery was a very puzzling question. The Captain and the Flight Engineer had been seen on a number of L-1011s, but most often on Plane 318. Why so often on that particular ship? A possible answer was soon found.

It was an answer that went back to something that had been done soon after the crash in the Florida Everglades. Work crews had gone over the wrecked L-1011. They had found some of the ship's gear to be undamaged. It was still in good working order. Among the undamaged gear were radios, compasses, instrument dials, and galley equipment. Eastern Airlines had removed these items and had placed them for further use in its other L-1011s, *chief among them Plane 318.* It had been perfectly safe to do this because none of the items had anything to do with the structural parts of the planes. But it certainly seemed that the spirits of the Captain and the Flight Engineer had followed all the pieces of equipment to their new homes.

For a time, something else puzzled everyone. The two ghosts were also seen on flights of another airline, TWA. But then it was found that all these appearances took place on L-1011s that TWA leased from Eastern for use during especially busy times of the year. Plane 318 was among the leased ships.

People who believe in ghosts do not think it strange that the spirits of the two men were seen around the equipment from the crashed plane. This is because of a theory they have about some ghosts.

It concerns the fact that we humans are much made up of electrical energy. The theory holds that this energy gives off great blasts of heat when a person dies violently, as in an accident. The heat remains in the area where the death occurred — and in the things to be found in that area. It is then seen in the form of "ghosts."

The theory may be a good one. Ghosts have been seen — or their presence felt — in houses and buildings in various parts of the world. Very often, it's been found that these houses and buildings were the scenes of unhappy lives, fights, murders, or accidental deaths.

The theory looks especially good in the case of the crashed L-1011. The accident, as you know, took place in December, 1972. The ghostly appearances began some weeks later. They continued throughout 1973. They became fewer and fewer in 1974. They finally stopped late that year. They became fewer in number when a troubled Eastern Airlines began removing the crashed airliner's equipment from Plane 318 and the other L-1011s. They stopped once all the equipment had been removed.

If you've found this story interesting, you'll enjoy reading a book called *The Ghost of Flight 401.* Written by John G. Fuller, it tells of the appearances you've read about in this chapter, plus many more.

At the start of his book, Mr. Fuller makes it clear that he once doubted that there are such things as ghosts. By the last chapter, after he has talked with the many airline people who saw the ghostly appearances, he seems to be changing his mind. He has found all the workers to be sensible people. He is certain that they weren't just "seeing things."

And, now, what about you?

Do you believe in ghosts? Do you believe that, on leaving this life, human beings go to a hereafter? Do you believe that the spirits of the dead can come to us from the hereafter? Or send us messages from there? Do you believe that a great discharge of heat can cause the spirit of a person to remain in the place where he or she died or among the things to be found in that place?

Or don't you believe in ghosts? And, if you don't, are you perhaps beginning to change your mind after reading about the Captain and the Flight Engineer?

3

THE MYSTERY
CLOUDS

Ghosts are more than mysterious. But they are not the only baffling things in the sky. Even the clouds have stories to tell. They've been the cause of several aviation mysteries.

For instance, look at what happened to the private plane that took off from Corpus Christi, Texas, on a summer day in 1930. With five businessmen aboard, if climbed into a sky that was clear except for a great dark cloud some miles away. Farmers were working their fields down below. They glanced up in time to see the plane disappear into the cloud.

A moment later, they were gasping with horror. The plane came tumbling out of the cloud. One wing was already ripped away. The other tore loose. Then the gasoline tanks broke free. The fuselage crashed into a nearby field. All five businessmen aboard were killed.

To this day, no one knows exactly what happened to the doomed ship while it was inside the cloud. Some farmers said that they heard an explosion just before they saw the plane drop into view. They felt that it had been hit by lightning. But there was a problem with that idea. There hadn't been a sign of thunder and lightning in the area all day long. And, except for the dark cloud, the weather was summery clear.

Others thought that perhaps the gasoline tanks had exploded. But this idea came to nothing. The ship hadn't been on fire when it dropped out of the cloud. And the tanks had been seen to fall away from the fuselage. Further, when the wreckage was examined, it bore no sign of fire. The absence of fire also indicated that lightning could not have been the cause.

And so the mystery remains. What had the plane run into up there in the cloud? There is no answer.

A Similar Crash

In that same year, 1930, a similar crash occurred in a cloud over the county of Kent in England. A private plane carrying six passengers took off. It flew into a cloud. A moment later, a number of people on the ground saw the ship plummet into view and spin to earth, killing all the passengers. One wing and the tail section floated down behind it.

Some witnesses said that they had heard an explosion while the plane was in the cloud. The idea that it had been hit by lightning was considered. But the wreckage, as in the Texas crash, showed no signs of fire.

A government investigation was conducted for several months. The investigation concluded with the guess that heavy winds inside the cloud had torn the tail section away. The investigators said that the explosion was probably caused by the sound of the tail and the wings tearing loose. But all this was theory only. The actual cause of the tragedy has never been learned.

Another Ghost Story?

One of the strangest of the cloud mysteries took place in 1961. It's very much like a ghost story and it began when a pilot was out for a day in his private plane. The sky above his Ohio home was filled with thick, white clouds. He swept through one, came out into a patch of blue, and—

The man caught his breath. There was another plane right in front of him. It was moving slowly and he was hurtling straight at its tail. He had just seconds to avoid a midair crash. Over hard went the controls. His plane banked sharply away. He missed smashing directly into the other ship. But he didn't miss it altogether. There was a grinding sound as

the tip of one silver wing scraped along its side.

The frightened pilot kept his plane from going into a dive. He looked back. He expected to see the other ship spinning earthward. But no. It was still there, bouncing slowly along on the wind. It was all right. Now his eyes widened. He saw that it was an old plane. It had two wings, spoked wheels, and an open cockpit. The pilot guessed that it was at least fifty years old. That meant that it had been around even before World War I.

The flyer couldn't believe what he was seeing. He knew of no fellow pilots who had a plane of this sort. Perhaps his eyes were playing tricks on him. He blinked. When he looked again, he knew he wasn't seeing things. The plane was the same as before — a real old-timer. He could make out the pilot. The fellow was wearing large goggles and a

In 1961, a pilot almost crashed into a plane from yesteryear. How did the old plane come to be in the air that day?

leather helmet. That sort of gear hadn't been worn for years.

As the pilot watched, the old ship banked away. It flew into a cloud and disappeared.

Shaken by the near disaster, the pilot headed back to his home field. On landing, he told the airport people of what had happened. He wanted to know who was up there in such a slow-moving, rickety old crate. It was a danger to all air traffic. The airport people said that no such plane had taken off from their field that day. They checked the surrounding fields. From each they got the same answer. No one knew a thing about the old ship and its goggled pilot.

The Ohio flyer shook his head. He knew that he had just lived through the most puzzling experience of his life. He wondered if he would ever solve the mystery.

The mystery *was* solved some months later — but the solution created an even greater mystery. At that time, some people accidentally came upon an ancient plane in a barn not far from the pilot's airfield. It was coated with dust and covered over with hay.

In every way, it matched the description of the ship that the pilot had hit with his silver wingtip. But there was one problem. It was obvious to everyone who saw the plane that it had been long in the barn and hadn't been flown for years.

Then something else happened. The logbook belonging to the old ship's pilot was found. In the last entry made in the book, the pilot told of a terrible experience. He had been flying in the clouds and, on coming out, had seen a big silver aircraft heading straight at him. The silver plane had turned quickly away, but not fast enough to keep its wingtip from scraping along the side of his ship. He had managed to keep his plane under control. On looking over his shoulder, he had seen the silver plane disappear into a cloud.

This last — and astonishing — entry had been made in the logbook fifty years earlier.

Aviation authorities checked the book closely. They determined it to be authentic. The old plane was just as thoroughly checked. On its side was found a long scrape mark. The mark contained bits of aluminum and silver paint. They were tested in a laboratory. They matched perfectly with aluminum and paint taken from the Ohio pilot's ship.

What had happened up there in the clouds? As some people believed, was it all a trick that the Ohio pilot had dreamed up to get his name in the newspapers? His friends and fellow pilots all said that he wasn't the type to pull such a stunt.

Or had he run into a ghost? Or had he and the old-time flyer been caught up in some sort of "time mishap"? Had he somehow gone back in time while the pilot of yesteryear had come forward in time, with the result that their paths finally crossed in one terrible moment?

Who can answer a question such as this? No one.

The Tunnel Cloud

Nor can anyone answer the question of what actually happened to a businessman as he was flying his private plane — a Beechcraft Bonanza — above the Atlantic Ocean one day. The year was 1970. The pilot was on his way from the Bahama Islands to Florida.

The Bonanza had been in the air just a few minutes when the man sighted a large cloud up ahead. He decided to climb above it. But, when he nosed upward, the cloud rose with him. It moved toward him. He climbed higher. But still the cloud came at him. There seemed no way to escape the thing. It closed around him.

The pilot later said that the cloud formed a tunnel around him. Strange things began happening. His instruments went out. The ship gained speed. Shaking from nose to tail, it seemed to be flung forward at a dizzying rate. The walls of the tunnel swept by on both sides.

Fighting the controls, the flyer kept the Bonanza on an even keel. He struggled all the while to break free of the tunnel. At last, after long minutes, he escaped and found blue sky everywhere. He sighed with relief.

Then his relief changed to astonishment. Dead ahead was the Florida coastline. He could see the city of Miami. He checked his watch. He had been in the air just 45 minutes. The flight from the Bahamas usually took about 90 minutes. Caught in the strange cloud tunnel, he had made the trip in half that time.

He shook his head. His Bonanza was fast — but not fast enough to do what it had done. The whole thing was impossible. But it had happened. He would never forget *that* fact to the end of his days.

And so what is there up inside the clouds that has played such tricks on a number of flyers? Did lightning cause the two planes to crash back there in 1930? Or did they run into some strange force that we know nothing about as yet — an invisible force that tore their wings away and sent them plummeting earthward. And is it a force that can alter time? A force that can send a modern plane back in time and a plane of yesteryear forward in time so that the two of them meet? A force that can whip a plane along at such a speed that it completes a journey in an impossibly short time?

Who knows?

The pilot who was caught in the cloud tunnel was flying over an especially strange area at the time — the stretch of ocean that is known as the Bermuda Triangle. It's been the scene of many aviation mysteries. We'll be talking about them later. But, first, let's turn to yet another cloud mystery — the puzzle of what happened to Airship L-8.

4

WHAT HAPPENED
TO AIRSHIP L-8?

Actually, this great "cloud mystery" doesn't concern an airplane. Rather, it centers around a U.S. Navy blimp known as Airship L-8. The mystery began to take shape at dawn on August 16, 1942. That was when the L-8 cleared its moorings at Treasure Island, the naval base in the middle of San Francisco Bay, and headed west on a routine flight.

At the controls in the gondola were Lt. (jg) Ernest Cody and Ens. Charles E. Adams. The gondola was a small cabin attached to the underside of the blimp. The two officers flew across the Bay and passed over the Golden

The L-8 just before one of her patrol flights during World War II.

Gate Bridge. To their left, the city of San Francisco lay under fog. The sky was overcast. Now and again, raindrops spattered against the windows of the gondola.

Cody and Adams were on a patrol flight. Now that the United States had been plunged into World War II, they had the job of checking for enemy submarines just off the northern California coast. But not a Japanese submarine had been sighted in U.S. coastal waters for months. And so the mission promised to be an uneventful one.

It turned out to be anything but uneventful. No one who played a part in the drama of that August day will ever forget it.

Once the L-8 had cleared the Golden Gate Bridge, it headed out over the Pacific Ocean. Two hours later—at 8:00 A.M.—it was a few miles from the Farallons, a group of small rocky islands about 30 miles out from San Francisco. Lieutenant Cody reached for his microphone and sent a radio message back to his base.

Going in for a Closer Look

Cody reported that he had sighted something on the ocean surface. It seemed to be

Lt. Ernest Cody

an oil slick. It might be coming from a
Japanese submarine. He said that he was
taking the L-8 down for a closer look. It was
the last time that his voice was heard.

55

Two fishing boats were at work nearby. Their crews saw the L-8 come out of a darkish cloud. They watched the airship as it went into a pattern of wide circles that brought it closer and closer to the sea. The fishermen knew that the Navy was always on the lookout for enemy subs. They were sure that the L-8 was after one now. They decided that they had better move their boats to a safer distance in case the airship started to drop its cargo of depth bombs.

The fishermen later said that the L-8 came out of its circling pattern at a height of about 300 feet. It hovered there in the mist for a moment. Then it moved forward over a stretch of water. But no depth bombs were dropped. Instead, causing the fishermen to gape with surprise, the airship suddenly bounced upward. It rose swiftly and disappeared back into the darkish cloud.

The blimp's disappearance was also seen ·by two patrol boats — one from the Coast Guard and the other from the Navy. They were closing in fast on the area. After receiving Lieutenant Cody's message, the Navy had sent them out to lend a hand in case the L-8 ran into a sub rather than a harmless oil slick.

The Silent Radio

Even though they had sent the patrol boats out, the radiomen back at base hadn't been worried by Lieutenant Cody's message. Oil slicks were always being sighted just off the coast. This would prove to be just another one. The radiomen were certain that Cody would soon tell them that all was well. But 15 minutes passed without a word from him. A call was sent to the blimp. There was no answer. Another call went out. Again, there was only silence.

The radiomen felt the first stirrings of worry. Had the L-8 come up against an enemy sub after all? Or had it gone down so low that it had crashed into the sea? Or had it simply experienced a radio failure? There was only one way to find out. Two rescue planes—

OS2U Kingfishers — were sent to the area.

The mystery deepened throughout the next two hours. The patrol boats radioed that they had seen the L-8 rise back into the dark cloud — and had not sighted it since. The Kingfishers reported that they were searching the seas near the Farallons. They couldn't see a trace of the blimp in the heavy clouds and mist. Then, at 10:30 A.M., a message came in from a Pan American Airways passenger plane. Its crew had caught a fleeting glimpse of the L-8. The blimp had been floating in and out of the clouds a few miles south of the Golden Gate Bridge.

Incident at the Beach

Two men had been spending the morning surf fishing on a beach just to the south of San Francisco. At 10:45 A.M., they looked up to see the L-8 come drifting in from the sea.

A news photographer caught this picture of the L-8 just before it crashed in Daly City, California.

58

The blimp was low over the water and seemed to be floating along under no control. Its mooring lines hung down from the nose. They scraped along the tops of the breakers and then were dragged along the sand.

The two fishermen grabbed the lines. They tried to pull the blimp down to the beach so that it would not crash into the cliffs behind them. They almost succeeded, only to have a gust of wind strike the blimp and send it scudding skyward. The men were dragged along the sand and then left behind. The L-8 cleared the cliffs and faded into the mist.

As they lay sprawled on the sand, the two men stared at each other in bewilderment. The door of the gondola had been open. They had gotten a look inside the small cabin as they had struggled with the ropes. It had been empty.

The strange flight of the L-8 ended a few minutes later. At a little past 11:00 A.M., with its air bag deflating, the blimp came down on a street in Daly City, which is located just south of San Francisco.

But the mystery was far from over. Navy authorities rushed to the crash site. They found everything in the gondola to be as it should be. The radio was in working order. Parachutes and a rubber life raft were stored in their proper places. The motors had stopped running, but there was nothing amiss with them. Only one thing was wrong— Lieutenant Cody and Ensign Adams were nowhere to be found.

What Had Happened?

What had happened to the two men? A team of Navy investigators tried to answer that question in the next months. The investigators considered all possibilities. They started with the idea that the L-8 had run into an enemy sub after leaving the area of the oil slick. The sub had taken the officers prisoners and then had released the blimp.

But there were shakes of the head. Like all blimps, the L-8 moved at a slow speed. It couldn't have gotten too far away from the

The wreckage of the L-8 lies in the street following its crash in Daly City. Note the section of the tail resting against a car.

four boats that had seen it circle the oil slick. The boats would have sighted it coming down again and running into a sub.

All right. Then perhaps the two officers were tossed out of the gondola when the blimp bounced back up and into the dark cloud. But no. It was known that they were wearing bright yellow life jackets during the flight. The crews of the watching boats would have seen flashes of yellow as the men fell. They would have glimpsed splashes when the two struck the water. And, even if no one had actually seen the fall, the jackets would have been easy to pick out on the surface of the sea. Any of the boats could have sighted them in the next hours.

There was yet another possibility. Perhaps some natural force had been lurking inside the cloud. Perhaps lightning. Perhaps a mighty gust of wind. Perhaps some force unknown to mankind. It had struck the L-8 and had thrown the two officers out through the open door of the gondola.

Again, there were shakes of the head, this

time at the idea of lightning. No thunder storms had been reported in the area that day. Further, the blimp showed no signs of the burns that lightning would have left behind.

As for a force unknown to man...well, who could say?

But a strong gust of wind. That seemed to be a real possibility. The investigators agreed that, sometime after leaving the area of the oil slick, the blimp must have been thrown over on its side by a blast of wind. One of the officers may have been standing by the open door at the time. He had lost his balance and had started to fall out. His companion had jumped to his aid. Both men had tumbled through the door and had plunged to the sea. They had been out of sight of the four boats and had drowned.

Yes. That was probably it. The explanation

Navy personnel looked closely at the gondola of the L-8 soon after the crash. To this day, no one knows what happened to the two Navy officers.

made sense. But no one knew for certain if it had an ounce of truth to it.

Today, only two things can be said for sure about the L-8 mystery. First, the ocean all along the coast near San Francisco was searched for long days. Nothing of Lieutenant Cody and Ensign Adams — neither their bodies nor their life jackets — was ever found. They had vanished without a trace.

Second, in all the long years since that fateful day in 1942, the Navy has never been able to solve the riddle of the L-8. It is a cloud mystery that will likely go on being a mystery for all time to come.

5

THEY DISAPPEARED

Throughout the early years of aviation, many pilots attempted long-distance
flights. These pilots—both men and women—
were daring people, but they were out for
something more than adventure. They were
testing stronger and stronger planes and were
trying to show that one day passengers could
travel safely by air to any part of the world.
They were among the many pioneers of today's
commercial aviation.

All the early long-distance flights add up to
a record of great achievement. They began on
July 15, 1909, when a French airman named

Louis Blériot took off from Calais, France. Sitting in the open cockpit of a tiny one-winger (a monoplane) that weighed just 661 pounds, he made his way to Dover, England. His flight, covering a distance of little more than 20 miles, marked the first air crossing of the English Channel. Blériot's mileage may not sound like much today, but it looked like a great deal back in 1909.

A decade later — in June, 1919 — two English pilots tried a much longer across-the-water journey. They flew a British bomber — a Vickers Vimy — from Canada's Newfoundland to Ireland. The 1,900-mile trip won John Alcock and Arthur Brown the honor of being the first men to fly the Atlantic Ocean nonstop. A month earlier, a group of American seaplanes had made an Atlantic crossing, but not a nonstop one. They flew from Newfoundland to the Azores Islands. From there, the flight took them to Portugal.

Next, in the spring of 1925, four U.S. Army Air Corps bombers left Seattle, Washington. After traveling over 26,000 miles, they

68

Frenchman Louis Blériot standing in his plane after making the first flight across the English Channel.

returned in 175 days. They were the first aircraft ever to circle the globe.

Charles A. Lindbergh thrilled the world in 1927 when he took off from Long Island, New York, and landed 33 hours later in Paris,

A welcoming crowd greets the "Spirit of St. Louis" and Charles Lindbergh on his arrival in Paris.

France. To him went the honor of being the first pilot to fly solo across the Atlantic. Another American, Amelia Earhart, became the first woman to solo the Atlantic when she flew her Lockheed Vega from Newfoundland to Ireland in 1932.

These have been just a few of the early long-distance flights. Altogether, dozens were attempted. They were all dangerous, made as they were without today's advanced equipment, and often without even radio gear aboard. Many ended in tragedy, with the flyers going down into the sea or crashing in an unexplored land area. Some of the crashes rank among the great mysteries of aviation because the pilots were never seen again. No one has ever been able to say what happened to them.

Nungesser and Coli

One of the earliest disappearances dates back to May 8, 1927. On that day, two French airmen — Charles Nungesser and Francois Coli — left Paris on a transatlantic flight. Great crowds were on hand to watch their ship fade into the distance. A few hours later, the crew of a freighter sighted it out over the Atlantic.

Nungesser and Coli in their plane just before their ill-fated flight across the Atlantic. What happened to them is still a mystery.

The plane was never seen again.

Since they carried no radio, the two flyers were unable to transmit their location at the time they went down. Perhaps they came down in the sea and drowned. Perhaps they got as far as their destination, Canada, and then crashed in a remote forested area, either dying in the smash-up or starving to death as they tried to find their way out of the woods. There is no way of telling.

One strange story indicates that the Frenchmen may have reached Canada. Some months after the pair had disappeared, a Canadian trapper came out of the woods. He showed the police a piece of paper he had found. It contained an SOS message that was signed "Nungesser." The message said that he and Coli had come down somewhere in the northern wilds.

The message was later given to Nungesser's mother. She said that the handwriting seemed to be that of her son. But the grammar used in the message was poor. The woman did not think that Nungesser

Charles Nungesser (left) and Francois Coli

would write in such a way. And so nothing was solved. Everyone wondered if the message was the "real thing" or a hoax played by the trapper to gain public attention.

And not a thing has been solved to this day. There have always been rumors, however, that Nungesser and Coli did indeed reach the Canadian wilds and were then held prisoner for long years by a remote tribe of Indians. But these are rumors, nothing more.

Partly Solved

One of the early disappearances was at least partly solved. It concerned the flight of Frederick Minchin and Leslie Hamilton. They took off from their native England in 1929 and headed for Canada. Riding with them as a passenger was the wealthy Princess Lowenstein-Wertheim of Germany. At age sixty-two, she had financed the journey and had insisted that she go along. Her great ambition was to be known as the first woman to fly the Atlantic.

Minchin and Hamilton, with their passenger sitting behind them in a specially built wicker chair, flew out over the ocean. They were sighted by several freighters and fishing boats. Then they disappeared.

The mystery of what had happened to the trio filled the newspapers in Europe and the United States for several weeks. Then pieces of a crashed plane were found just off the coast of Iceland. Among the wreckage was the wicker chair belonging to the Princess. Part of the mystery had been solved. But not the rest of it. Had the three crash victims drowned in the freezing North Atlantic? Or had they made it to shore and then died of exposure and starvation? The bodies were never found and so these questions have remained unanswered ever since.

But, as had happened in the Nungesser disappearance, an odd story came out during the search for the lost aircraft. A Canadian lighthouse keeper reported that one night he had seen the lights of an airplane overhead. His lighthouse, standing on the coast of Labrador, was along the route of the Minchin-Hamilton flight. But it seemed impossible that he had seen their ship because the sighting was made long after they would have run out of fuel. Yet, when an effort was made to locate some local pilot who might have been out that night, no one could be found.

So what had the lighthouse keeper really seen? Some unknown plane? Or the Minchin-

Hamilton ship? And, if it was their plane, how had it managed to stay aloft for so long after running out of fuel? And how had it then managed to get clear back to Iceland before crashing?

Questions. Questions. But no answers.

Solved!

The Atlantic claimed many a victim from among the pilots who early attempted to cross it, as did the Pacific when the first flights over its vast waters were tried. Old-time pilots will never forget what happened to the planes that tried to race from California to Hawaii in 1927. Three of the ships were lost at sea while another five crashed on takeoff or landing. Not one of the lost racers was ever found.

But it must be said that the *very first* disappearance on an over-the-ocean flight was quickly solved — and in a way that delighted the world. The story takes us clear back to 1919.

It was May 18. John Alcock and Arthur

Brown were planning to fly the Atlantic in another few weeks. (Their journey, as you'll remember, would end in success.) Those four American bombers were already over the ocean. After a stopover in the Azores Islands, they were due to arrive in Portugal at the end of the month. But today, on the 18th, the well-known British test pilot Harry Hawker and his friend Kenneth Mackenzie-Grieve were out to beat them all to the punch. They were determined to be the first men across the Atlantic. Climbing into a Sopwith biplane, they took off from Newfoundland on a nonstop hop to England.

The flight was supposed to take a day to complete. When the pair failed to arrive in England on time, the world went into mourning for them. No one doubted that the two flyers had crashed somewhere in the Atlantic and had drowned. They would never be heard from again.

For seven days, the sad story of the doomed pair was on the front pages of newspapers in all countries. Then, suddenly, all was changed from gloom to jubilation. A Danish freighter sailed into an English port. Hawker and Mackenzie-Grieve were alive and on board. And their plane was securely lashed to the deck. The Sopworth had, indeed, gone down in the Atlantic. But, with the two flyers clinging to it, the little ship had remained afloat. The passing Danish freighter had sighted them and had plucked them from the freezing waters.

Hawker and Mackenzie-Grieve had made it across the Atlantic, all right. But not as planned.

The long-distance flights, claiming the lives of so many fine pilots and leaving us with so many mysterious disappearances, finally led us to the age of commercial aviation. That age dawned in the 1930s. There was now airmail and passenger service throughout the United States and in many other countries. There were airliners making their way across the Atlantic. There were giant flying clippers traveling above the Pacific.

And there was the woman flyer who gave the world one of the greatest and most puzzling of aviation mysteries. Her name: Amelia Earhart.

6

THE VANISHED ELECTRA

It was early 1937. Just five years ago, Amelia Earhart had become the first woman to solo the Atlantic. Now she was out to capture an even greater prize. She tried to become the first woman to circle the globe. The effort ended when her Lockheed Electra ground-looped on takeoff from Hawaii. Gasoline splashed over the runway. There was the great danger of fire. But no flames burst from the ship. The slender flyer climbed unhurt from the pilot's cabin.

Three months later, with her ship repaired, Earhart tried again. She was thirty-nine years

Amelia Earhart

old at the time. Starting from the United States, she and her navigator, Fred Noonan, flew down the east coast of South America. They refueled and crossed the Atlantic to Africa. From there, they made their way over the Indian Ocean to India. The next leg took them to Singapore. Throughout the month-long adventure, the whole world watched and waited for every scrap of news on how the two flyers were faring.

At last, Earhart and Noonan put the Electra down for refueling on the island of New Guinea in the Pacific. More than half their journey was behind them. But facing them now was the long jump to Howland Island.

The pilot and her navigator knew that the most dangerous part of their trip lay ahead. Howland was a tiny dot in the sea, 2,556 miles away. There would be no landmarks to guide them along their way—only vast stretches of ocean. For much of the hop, they would be too far out for radio contact with either New Guinea behind them or Howland up ahead. Noonan would have to keep them on course by sighting

Amelia Earhart stands by while navigator Fred Noonan climbs aboard the Electra during their attempt to circle the globe.

on the stars and the sun. If the sky clouded over, he wouldn't be able to do so. The risk of flying off course and missing Howland was great.

A miss promised almost certain death. The Electra would run out of fuel and plunge into the sea. Searchers would have a hard time finding it in the vast Pacific wastes.

The Flight to Howland

Despite all the danger, Earhart and Noonan took off out over the ocean on July 2, 1937. They had one great hope. The U.S. Coast Guard cutter *Itasca* was on patrol a few miles off Howland. It had a powerful radio aboard. Along with the radio station on the island itself, the cutter was to contact Earhart as soon as she was within range. Then it would guide her in.

Earhart flew east through the day and into the night. By midnight, the *Itasca's* radio operator was sure that she must be within range. He began calling her, but received no answers. Finally, just before 3:00 A.M., a call came from the Electra. Through heavy static, the operator heard Earhart say that the weather was cloudy. Oh-oh! Clouds meant that Noonan would have a hard time guiding the plane by the stars. The operator tried a return call. There was no reply. Obviously, the pilot couldn't yet hear him.

Throughout the rest of the night, the *Itasca* received calls from Earhart. Each time, the ship radioed back. Each time, there was no reply. And, each time, the ship and the station on Howland tried to get a radio fix on the Electra so that they could tell the flyer where she was — that is, if any of their calls ever got through. Every attempt failed. The ship sent out homing signals to guide the Electra to its destination. Earhart's calls made no mention of them. They were going unheard. Something must be wrong with her radio receiver. Clouds and a bad receiver! The pilot was almost certain to wander off course.

Further calls came from the Electra with the dawn. It was now clear that Earhart had indeed lost her way. She said that she could not see Howland, but felt certain that it must be nearby. She added that the Electra was running low on fuel. It could stay aloft just a few hours more. On a 9:00 A.M. call, she

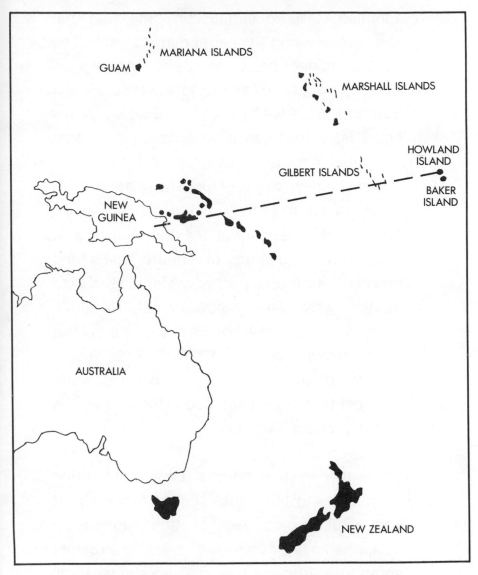

The route from New Guinea to Howland Island

sounded close to exhaustion. She said that she was waiting for a homing signal. The *Itasca* radioed back. More homing signals were sent. There were no replies. Amelia Earhart's voice was never heard again. A few hours later, the men on the *Itasca* knew that she must now have run out of fuel.

Immediately, Navy ships and planes were called in for a search of the South Pacific. The search lasted for more than two weeks. It covered thousands of square miles and reached into the Gilbert and Marshall islands to the west and northwest of Howland. Nothing was found — not a trace of the Electra or the flyers, not a sign of wreckage, not a glimpse of a life jacket. A saddened world was told that the Pacific had claimed the lives of the woman flyer and her navigator.

But —

A great many people could not bring themselves to think that such a famous pilot had actually died. As so often happens in disappearance cases, all sorts of rumors sprang up — rumors that insisted she was still alive. One held that Earhart and Noonan were in love and had flown off to live on some South Pacific island. In light of her calls to the *Itasca*, this idea was sheer nonsense. The calls could leave no doubt that she had been desperately trying to find Howland.

Then another rumor took shape. It is one that has persisted to this day.

On a Government Mission?

At the time of the Electra's disappearance, the United States felt certain that Japan was preparing for World War II. Our government suspected the Japanese were building fortifications on the many islands they held in the South Pacific, among them the Marshall Islands to the northwest of Howland. If so, they were violating an international peace agreement. And so the rumor broke out that officials in Washington, D.C., had asked Earhart to make a detour over the Marshalls while flying to Howland. She was then to report what she had seen.

The rumor had it that she had made the detour. She had then run out of fuel or had been forced down by Japanese gunfire. Another version of the rumor said that she had strayed far off course to the Marshalls and had met the same fate. Each rumor went on to say that she was being held prisoner by the Japanese.

No one knows if these rumors have any truth to them. But, over the years, a number of strange stories have come out of the South Pacific. They're stories that have placed Earhart and Noonan — or people who looked like them — in the Marshalls at about the time of their disappearance.

For instance, in the days following World War II, a native woman living on one of the Marshalls told the Americans there of something she had seen as a child. She said that a plane had crashed in the sea near her home. Japanese soldiers had gone out and fetched two white people ashore — a man and a woman. The native said that the woman had been dressed in khaki slacks and had worn her hair cut short. It was a description that fitted Earhart. The two strangers had then been sent to a Japanese base in the Marianas, a group of islands to the west of the Marshalls.

Additional stories came from the island of Saipan in the Marianas. One native woman related how, as a girl, she had seen a plane crash in the harbor there. Two white people — again, a woman and a man — had come ashore under the guard of Japanese soldiers. Again, the woman was dressed in khaki and wore her hair cut short.

Those who heard the story wondered if the crashed plane was the one that had brought Earhart and Noonan from the Marshalls. Or was it, perhaps, the Electra flying far off course? Or perhaps it was a plane flown by whites from some distant island not in Japanese hands.

In finishing her story, the Saipan native said that the white woman had been held captive. The man had been executed as a spy. Others said that the woman had later died of dysentery. Still others said that both the man and woman had been executed.

Topping off all these stories were claims made by several American soldiers during World War II. They said that, while fighting to wrest the Marshalls from the Japanese, they had come upon photographs of Earhart. In one, she was seen standing with a Japanese army officer. Some of the photographs were turned over to the U.S. military authorities. Others were lost in combat.

Are the Stories True?

Many people believe the various stories. Just as many don't. There is no way of knowing who is right. This is because there is no way of proving the accuracy of the stories.

For example, take the islanders who claimed to have seen the white captives. No one doubts that they were telling the truth. But they told their stories in the mid-1940s, years after seeing the two. Some could not be sure that 1937 was the year of the prisoners' arrival. The memory clouds over after such a long time. The prisoners, then, could have been seen in some other year — perhaps 1936 or 1938.

Further, it is possible that the captives were flyers other than Earhart and Noonan. The description of the white woman fitted Earhart, true. But many women pilots wore khaki outfits. Nor was it unusual for a woman to wear her hair cut short.

On top of all else, there was a goodly amount of island-to-island flying being done at the time. It's possible that some plane had wandered off course from a group of distant islands and had blundered into Japanese territory. And possible that some plane, piloted by actual spies, had indeed flown in for a look at the Japanese fortifications. And also possible that Earhart, either far off course or on a mission for her government, was at the controls. Who can tell?

And what of the photographs? They add up to a real mystery. Over the years, they've disappeared into government files or have been lost. The people who are interested in the Earhart case have never been able to see them.

Many people suspect that both the Japanese and United States governments know that the two flyers were taken prisoner. But neither government is willing to discuss the case. It is felt that the Japanese government will not talk because of the embarrassment of admitting that its soldiers once held the pair and either executed them or allowed them to die. It is also felt that the U.S. government will not speak out for fear of embarrassing and angering a one-time enemy that is now a close friend.

And so the question of what happened to Amelia Earhart and Fred Noonan remains a mystery, more than forty years after they set out over the sea for tiny Howland Island. Did they deliberately make a detour to check the Marshalls for the government? Did they wander so far off course that they finally entered Japanese territory? Or, in their search for Howland, did they at last run out of fuel and fall into the sea?

It's a mystery that may never be solved.

7
THE DEADLY
TRIANGLE

It was just before ten o'clock on a night in February. Lights from nearby hotels glimmered on the Atlantic surf as it rolled up on the sands of Daytona Beach, a popular resort area in Florida. Hundreds of people strolled along the shore. They had come here to escape the winter cold up north and were now enjoying the mild, clear evening.

The sudden roar of a low-flying plane startled them. They looked up. What they saw froze them in their tracks. The plane was sweeping in from the sea, dropping lower and lower as it came. It seemed to be hurtling straight at the beach. Horrified, the people saw it crash into the shallow water about 100 yards offshore.

Frantic calls went out to a nearby Coast Guard station. Within minutes, Coast Guard cutters were on the scene. They probed the waters with their searchlights as they swept back and forth out there just beyond the surf. In such shallow water, the wreckage should have been easy to locate. But the plane couldn't be found. It had disappeared, never to be seen again.

What had happened to the plane?

It seemed impossible that it could have been washed out to sea, not in such a short time and not without leaving some trace behind. Coast Guard officials began to wonder if the people strolling the beach had been "seeing things." But that seemed impossible, too. Hundreds said that they had seen the crash. Many of them were able to describe the plane. Their descriptions were all the same. It had been a private plane, silver with red-and-green wingtips.

But what had happened to it?

Not to this day has that question ever been answered.

The Deadly Triangle

The mysterious crash took place along the edge of one of the strangest ocean areas in the world — the great expanse of sunlit sea known as the Bermuda Triangle. For years now, it has been the scene of numerous puzzling incidents. The pilot who found himself caught in the "tunnel cloud" that was mentioned in Chapter 4 was flying over the Triangle at the time. Most of the incidents have been tragic disappearances. Sailboats, yachts, freighters, private airplanes, and airliners — all have been swallowed up by the Triangle and never seen again.

The Bermuda Triangle can be easily found on any map of the United States. Start on the stretch of Florida coast that runs from Daytona Beach down to Miami. Now move southeast across the Atlantic to the island of Puerto Rico. Next, move northward to Bermuda. Finally, return to your starting point

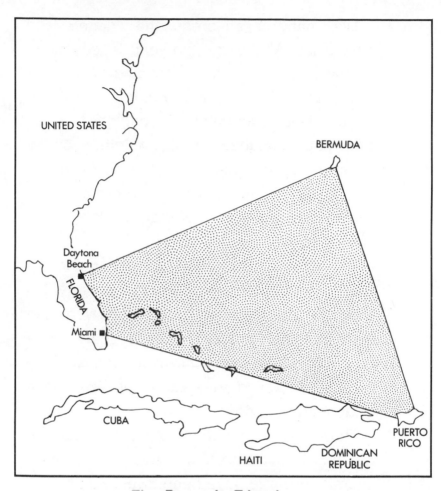

The Bermuda Triangle

on the Florida coastline. You'll have tracked your way around an ocean area of some 440,000 square miles.

Like many ocean areas, the Triangle is a busy place. All through the year, it sees much shipping, sports sailing, and air traffic. Most ships and planes pass through it without trouble. But an alarming number don't. Ships sink and airplanes crash in other ocean areas, of course, and are often never found. But the losses in the Triangle are more than seems normal — and certainly far more mystifying.

The earliest records of disappearances in the Triangle date back to the last century. It's known that at least six sailing ships vanished there in the 1800s. Four of them were American warships. In our own century, more than 40 seagoing vessels of all sizes have disappeared without a trace.

The silver plane crashed into the surf at Daytona Beach in 1935. It was one of three aircraft known to have been swallowed by the Triangle in the years before World War II. The number of disappearing planes has increased since the end of the war. Take 1945, for instance. That year alone saw three disappearances.

The Strange Events of 1945

The mysteries began in the summer. Twelve Navy bombers took off one day from Florida for a training flight over the Atlantic.

An Avenger torpedo bomber

They were gone for several hours. When they returned, only ten landed. Two were missing.

The pilots who had come safely home could not explain the loss of their companions. There had been times during the flight when all the planes were not in sight of each other. But none of the ten safe arrivals had received a radio message from the missing ships to say that they had run into trouble. Further, the weather conditions had been perfect. A storm hadn't knocked the pair out of the sky. Nor had there been any harsh winds to damage them. Nothing could explain the disappearance. The two had simply vanished. They were never found.

Next, in December of the year, a flight of five Navy planes headed out over the sea from Florida. They were TBM Avenger torpedo bombers. They, too, were on a training mission. They departed at two o'clock in the afternoon. Two hours later, the pilot commanding the flight radioed his base. His voice sounded confused. He said that he thought the planes were off course...he wasn't sure of his position...it was maybe some 200 miles northeast of the base...but he wasn't sure. He couldn't even tell which way was west. This was a very odd statement because the day was clear. It should have been easy for him to sight on the sun.

Then another pilot came on the radio. His voice was also confused. He said that the sea looked strange. Now came the oddest statement of all. The planes, he said, seemed to be heading into white water.

At that moment, the radios fell silent. The voices of the flyers were never heard again.

Immediately, the Navy sent a Mariner flying boat to the position given by the first pilot. Manned by twelve men, the Mariner was a plane designed for sea rescues. It reached its destination in 30 minutes. The pilot radioed the base. No sign of the bombers could be seen. He said that he was going to search the area for miles around. He clicked off his radio.

As things turned out, the missing bombers were never located, even though a search by Navy ships and planes lasted for long days and covered several thousand square miles. On a sunny December afternoon, the Triangle had recorded its second mysterious disappearance for 1945.

And, as things turned out, the year's third disappearance took place that very December afternoon. It came sometime after the Mariner pilot radioed that he was going to search the area. Once he'd clicked off his radio, he didn't call again. His plane vanished right along with the torpedo bombers. Like them, it was never found.

Though no one knows what happened to the torpedo bombers, there is a story that might explain the disappearance of the Mariner. A ship was sailing in the area at the time of the trouble. Its crew reported that they saw a flash of light just above the distant horizon. The Mariner had always had a problem with leaking fuel. Perhaps the leak filled the plane with fumes that day and caused it to explode. Perhaps the ship's crew had seen that explosion. Perhaps.

A Mariner flying boat like these went out to look for the vanished Avengers. It, too, disappeared.

But who can say? All that is known for certain is that the big Mariner disappeared right along with the bombers.

Other Mysteries

The disappearances in 1945 were mysterious, yes. But they were no more baffling than those that came in the next years.

For example, look what happened in 1948. An airliner, with 32 passengers aboard, was flying from Puerto Rico to Miami. The plane was a DC-3 and it cut smoothly through the night sky. At last, the Florida coastline came into view. The pilot radioed the Miami tower that he was just 50 miles away. He could see the lights of the city. The weather was fine. All was well on board. He'd be landing in a few minutes.

Like the Mariner pilot, he clicked off the radio. Like the Mariner pilot, he didn't call again. And, like the Mariner itself, his plane disappeared. It was never found — even though its last reported position was a scant 50 miles from its destination.

The DC-3 wasn't the only airliner to vanish in the Triangle. Two British passenger planes also disappeared, one in 1948 and the other in 1949. Both were never heard from again after sending radio messages that the weather was fine and that all was normal on board.

One of the most baffling stories concerns the private plane that was approaching a small island one day in 1962. The weather was sunny and clear. The pilot was within sight of the island and its airport. But he radioed a strange request. He asked for directions to the island. The tower called back with landing instructions. Then the people in the tower watched him circle offshore. He seemed unable to see a place that was clearly in view. At last, he flew back out to sea. He was never found.

Two giant KC-135 air tankers played the leading parts in another disappearance. They belonged to the U.S. Air Force. On the morning of August 28, 1963, the four-engined pair left Florida for a refueling exercise near Bermuda. At noon, they reported that they were about 300 miles west of Bermuda. They were flying together in clear weather.

After that one message, their radios fell silent. All efforts to contact the two failed. At last, worried Air Force officials sent several planes out to look for them. Nothing was found, but the next day the tower radio began to crackle with bad news. Wreckage had been sighted. It was in the sea a little less then 300 miles off Bermuda.

A Coast Guard cutter sped to the area. Its crew checked the wreckage closely. The twisted metal had once been a KC-135. What had happened seemed obvious. The two planes had collided in midair and had crashed into the sea. One had sunk. The other had been strewn over the surface.

Yes. It seemed obvious.

Or was it?

Two days later, more wreckage was found. It turned out to be the remains of one of the KC-135s. But there was a strange problem. This wreckage was found 160 miles away from the twisted metal of its sister ship.

So it appeared that the two planes hadn't

collided after all. The ocean currents couldn't have carried the wreckage of the second ship away so fast that the Coast Guard cutter wouldn't have seen it. Then what had actually happened out there over the sea? One baffling question after another came to mind.

If the KC-135s had suddenly collided, there would have been no time for an SOS message back to base. But, if just one had gone down at the site of the first crash, why hadn't its pilot radioed that he was in trouble? He would have had the time to do so. And why hadn't the other ship radioed that there was trouble? Were their radios on the blink? *Both* radios. It just didn't seem possible.

And if only one had crashed, why did the other fly on for another 160 miles in a direction away from its home base? Why hadn't it headed home with the bad news? And why no distress signal during those long miles?

But suppose the two *had* collided? Then how had one managed to fly on for 160 miles before falling into the sea? And, again, why no SOS? Was its radio out? Or was it caught in some force unknown to man?

These are questions that have never been answered. It is likely that they never will be.

As strange as they are, the disappearances are not the only mysteries that the Triangle has given us. There have been other odd incidents, such as that eerie "tunnel cloud." Pilots have lived through them and have puzzled over them for years afterward. Let's look now at some of these riddles. And then let's see if there's some cause behind all of the mysteries in the Triangle.

8

ARE THERE
ANSWERS?

It is said that more than 1,000 people in ships, sailing boats, and airplanes have disappeared in the Bermuda Triangle during the years since 1945. Only a fortunate few have lived through strange experiences and have escaped to tell of them. One such lucky survivor was the pilot who found himself being whirled along in that "tunnel cloud."

Another was Charles A. Lindbergh, the first man to solo the Atlantic. A few months after his great flight, he paid a visit to Cuba. When he was returning to the United States on a February night in 1928, he flew through a part

of the Triangle. Suddenly, his compasses began to misbehave. The needles flung themselves back and forth for no reason that he could see. His land indicator instrument also began to wobble. The puzzled Lindbergh had no choice but to guide himself by the stars. But he couldn't see them. They were covered by a haze.

At dawn, Lindbergh sighted a group of islands that he recognized. He shook his head. He had flown more than 300 miles off course. He banked and headed for Florida. His compasses and land indicator were still acting up. Then the coast of Florida passed beneath. At that moment, the compasses and indicator stopped giving him trouble. They worked properly for the rest of the trip. It was a strange incident that Lindbergh never forgot.

What happened to the crew of a U.S.

Soon after Charles A. Lindbergh became the first pilot to solo the Atlantic, he and his plane ran into strange trouble over the Bermuda Triangle.

bomber during World War II was more than strange. It was frightening. They were on their way from Florida to duty in Italy. The night air was calm as they put Bermuda behind them. Then it happened.

Without warning, they were struck by some terrific force. Their huge ship flipped over on its back. In an instant, it was turned right side up again. Then over on its back it went once more. Now it nosed into a dive and screamed toward the water. The pilot and copilot fought with the controls. Desperately, they tried to pull the plane up. Only in the last seconds before crashing did they succeed. The big ship straightened out when it was so close to the sea that the crew could make out the white tops of the waves.

Much the same thing happened to an airliner years later when it was flying in the same area. Suddenly, the plane dropped several hundred feet. It plunged downward with such force that the food trays on the passengers' laps were flung high — so high that they hit the ceiling. Then, for 15 minutes, the plane was tossed about as if it were in a storm.

But there was no storm. The air was calm and the weather clear — just as they had been on that frightening night back in World War II. A storm couldn't be blamed.

Then what was it that had hit the two planes?

Are There Answers?

People everywhere have long been fascinated by the mysteries of the Bermuda Triangle. No one, of course, has been able to solve the mysteries. But many have theories on what must be causing all the trouble. Among them are a number of scientists. When you listen to these people talk, you'll hear them mention five main theories.

The first holds that there must be a powerful magnetic force at work in the Triangle. What else, many people ask, could have thrown Lindbergh's compasses and land indicator out of kilter that night in 1928? It could have caused many pilots to become lost, with the result that they flew too far off course, ran out of fuel, crashed, and disappeared beneath the waves before anyone could find them. Also, many planes had their radios go dead just before vanishing. Such trouble could have been caused by strong magnetism.

If there is great magnetism in the Triangle, then where does it come from? Some scientists say that it could be caused by matter from outer space — perhaps meteors — that hit the earth millions of years ago, landing in the Triangle and elsewhere.

Elsewhere? Yes. The Triangle isn't alone in having magnetic problems. There are other areas where compasses, radios, and electrical equipment go awry. Including the Triangle, there are nine areas in all. They're located in a line that circles the globe near the equator. One, for instance is located in the Indian Ocean. Another lies in the Pacific Ocean south of Japan. Were all these areas once hit by matter from space? Or is there a strange belt of magnetism that girdles the world to either side of the equator?

More Theories

According to the next theory, there may be an odd atmospheric force present in the Triangle. It gives the air and sea an appearance that is confusing to pilots. Remember how one of the pilots with the five torpedo bombers said that the air and the ocean looked weird? Then he said the strangest thing of all — that the planes seemed to be flying into white water.

And remember the pilot who was caught in the "tunnel cloud"? And the KC-135 tanker that failed to see its sister ship crash into the water? And the plane that disappeared back out over the ocean when the pilot could not see an island that was almost beneath him? Could they have all been the victims of some mighty atmospheric force that made them "see things"? Or that made things invisible to them?

Next, many people believe that the

disappearances were caused by natural forces. It is known that the Triangle is an area of strong winds. These winds are usually found at high altitudes. They run in different directions. Suppose a plane is traveling with a wind that is moving in one direction. Then it is hit by a fierce wind from another direction. The force of that blow can be enough to shatter a small or medium-sized aircraft and send it plunging, in pieces, to the sea below.

The Triangle is also an area of waterspouts, which are great funnels of water that whip into the air. They are really tornadoes at sea and are caused when the winds collide from different directions. It is believed that they're responsible for the many ships and sailing boats that have disappeared in the Triangle over the years. They can rise high enough to catch a low-flying airplane. Some people suspect that the torpedo bomber pilot was seeing a waterspout when he radioed that his formation seemed to be flying into white water.

The Triangle, too, is an area of strong tides. There are great rocky caverns under the surface. The sea floor is made up of quicksand in many places. It is widely believed that these natural features are behind the fact that so many ships, boats, and airplanes have vanished without a trace. The tides carried them away before they could be found. Or their wreckage worked its way into some cavern and was forever hidden from view. Or it was swallowed up by the quicksand.

The Strangest Ideas

The final two theories are ones that can really stretch the imagination. One holds that there is a sort of "time doorway" in the Triangle. It's an invisible doorway that many ships and planes accidentally pass through. Once on the other side, they find themselves in some other world. Or in some other time dimension. In either case, they're never seen again. And they leave no trace of themselves.

The five torpedo bombers, the Mariner search plane, and the plane that crashed into the surf of Daytona Beach — could they have all passed through that "time doorway"?

The other theory is held by people who believe that Earth is being visited by life forms from other planets. They say that the alien visitors long ago decided to use the waters of the Triangle as a "collecting station." There, they pick up passing ships, boats, and planes. They take them away so that they can study their crews and passengers.

Do these last two theories make any sense at all? Perhaps. Perhaps not. Science is teaching us that time is, indeed, a strange thing and that we really know little about it. It may not be impossible that there are such things as "doorways" to other worlds and other time dimensions.

And what of visitors from space? For centuries now, mankind has sighted mysterious things in the sky. We in the twentieth century have come to call them "unidentified flying objects" — UFOs. There have been an especially large number of sightings over the years since World War II.

Some of the UFOs have been the result of natural causes, such as the gases that rise from swamps and appear as moving lights in the night sky. Some have been revealed as hoaxes. Not a few tricksters have produced photographs that were supposed to be of "flying saucers." They turned out to be pictures of such things as frisbees and the lids of tin cans. And some sightings have been of quite ordinary objects. For instance, there's the pilot who chased a UFO for miles only to find that it was a runaway weather balloon.

But many sightings have been real mysteries. A number of people have seen UFOs that can't be explained away as hoaxes or anything else. Take the airliner that was flying above the Pacific in the late 1940s. The passengers and crew looked out the windows to see what appeared to be a giant silver fish in the distance. It flew along with them for

Weather balloons have been mistaken for UFOs.

several minutes. Then it turned away and disappeared.

What sort of UFO were they seeing?

Perhaps a spaceship manned by visitors from another world?

If so, then it may be that we *are* being studied by extra-terrestrials. And it may be that they *have* established a "collecting station" in the Triangle.

There are millions of planets and stars in the universe. Our scientists are sure that some of them, along with Earth, must have life forms on them. Yet, would it be possible for them to travel to Earth? Many scientists don't think so. They feel that an impossible amount of energy and time would be needed to bring a spaceship from even the stars nearest to us.

But who can tell?

And so we're left only with questions. Is there a powerful magnetic force in the Bermuda Triangle? Are there weird atmospheric conditions there? Are the disappearances caused by natural forces? Is there a "time doorway" somewhere in those sunlit waters? Or is the Triangle a "collecting station" used by visitors from space?

Perhaps one day we'll know.

The history of aviation in our century has been a magnificent one. Over the years, it has sent all types of aircraft flying higher and faster and for greater and greater distances. But, as we've seen in this book, it has also been a history filled with mysteries that have no solution. It's given us one puzzling airplane story after another. With the skies being as endless as they are, it will likely go on doing so for all time to come.

INDEX

Adams, Charles E., 52-66
Air Force, U.S., 107-108
Airship L-8, 52-66
Alcock, John, 68, 77
Atlantic Ocean, first nonstop
    flight across the,
    68, 77-78

Balloons, weather, 121, 122
Beechcraft Bonanza, 49-50
Bermuda Triangle, 51,
    96-123
Biplane, German, 13-15
Blériot, Louis, 68, 69
Blimp, U.S. Navy (L-8), 52-66
British aircraft, 12-23
Brown, Arthur, 68, 77-78

California, 52-66
Canada, 16-17, 68, 73-75
Clouds, mystery, 10, 40-51,
    52-66

Coast Guard, U.S., 97
Cody, Ernest, 52-66
Coli, Francois, 71-75
Corpus Christi, Texas, 40

Daly City, California, 58,
    60-62
Daytona Beach, Florida, 96,
    100, 120

Earhart, Amelia, 70, 80,
    81-95
Eastern Airlines, ghosts of
    24, 25-39
Electra, 81-95
England, 12-23, 42-43
English Channel, 68
Everglades, 27, 35

"Flying saucers," 121
Fuller, John G., 38

125

German aircraft, 12-23
Ghost of Flight 401, The
(Fuller), 38
Ghost planes, 11, 45-48
of World War I and II,
12-23
Ghosts, 11, 14, 15, 23,
36-39, 40, 48
of Eastern Airlines, 24,
25-39

Hamilton, Leslie, 75-77
Handley Page bomber, 22
Hawker, Harry, 78-79
Heinkel bombers, 16
Henshaw, "Old Willie," 17-18
"Hot One, The," 20-23
Howland Island, 83-87, 89,
94, 95

Iceland, 76, 77
Iron Cross, 14
Itasca (U.S. Coast Guard
cutter), 85-86, 88, 89

Japan, 89-95

KC-135 air tankers, 107-110,
117
Kingfishers, 58

L-8, Airship, 52-66
L-1011s, 27-37
Lindbergh, Charles A.,
69-70, 111-113, 115
Lockheed Electra, 81-95
Lockheed L-1011, 27-37
Lowenstein-Wertheim,
Princess, 75-76

Mackenzie-Grieve, Kenneth,
78-79
Magnetism, 115-117, 123
Mariner flying boat, 103-105,
106, 120
Mexico City, 33, 34
Miami, Florida, 27, 50, 106
Minchin, Frederick, 75-77
Monoplane, 68
Mystery clouds, 10, 40-51,
52-66

Navy blimp, U.S. (L-8) 52-66
Noonan, Fred, 83-95
Nungesser, Charles, 71-75

Ohio, 43-48
"Old Willie," (ghost pilot),
16-18
OS2U Kingfishers, 58

Pan American Airways, 58
Pilots
disappearing, 71-80
Eastern Airlines, 29, 33,
34
German bomber, 18, 20,
23
ghost, 13, 17, 23, 45-46
Royal Air Force, 12-23
U.S. Navy, 102-104
Planes, ghost.
See Ghost planes

Quicksand, 119

"Spirit of St. Louis," 70
Spirits, 15, 36, 38

Spitfires, 16-17

TBM Avenger torpedo
   bombers, 102
Tides, in Bermuda Triangle
   area, 119
"Time doorway," 119-120,
   123
Treasure Island, (San
   Francisco Bay), 52
Tri-star Whisperliner, 27
"Tunnel cloud," 48-50, 117
TWA, 36

"Unidentified flying objects"
   (UFOs), 121-123

United States, and
   disappearance of
   Amelia Earhart, 89-95

Warsaw, Poland, 18-20
Waterspouts, 118
Weather balloons, 121, 122
"White Angel of Warsaw,"
   18-20
World War I, ghost planes
   of, 12-23
World War II
   Airship L-8, 52-66
   ghost planes of, 12-23
Wright Brothers (Wilbur and
   Orville), 25, 26